Day One Crazy

Felicity West

Day One Crazy

Felicity West

If you think you should have standards for yourself, love yourself, be confident, or be able to have independent thoughts, you must be CRAZY! …Well, at least in today's society.

This journal is for the goal getters and life livers of the world! It's for those of us that want more for ourselves than the status quo, or simply what's expected of us. We all have something we're passionate about; family, hobbies, career, money, travel, etc. This journal is designed to help you not only chart and plan, but to also encourage you to be crazy enough to believe and know you can do it!

And if you're going to be crazy you might as well start now.

Be Day One Crazy!

As you use your journal you may choose to do so daily, weekly, monthly or more. You can start it any month or day. Here are some helpful hints:

- Remember that this is just for you! Create your own brand of "Crazy" and give it to the world on Day One!

- Write a monthly mantra to help you stay in tune with your why; what is pushing you? Your monthly mantra can also serve as your daily affirmation.

- Each day (Sunday, Monday, etc.) has a suggested activity that will help create sustainable habits. When combined, they are all great lifestyle changes to incorporate as you see fit. Feel free to modify, ignore, or repeat to suit your goals.

- On the action diagram, don't feel overwhelmed to place something in each circle. Remember, this is just for you. If you don't feel the need to fill a circle any given month, don't! Also, feel free to repeat your actions month to month!

- When you complete the "For My" table write in things that you did or want to do for each of those areas in your life. Doesn't need to be complicated. Folding the laundry is a small yet big home victory. The idea is that small steps make a big difference!

- Make it your own! Enjoy your growth! Learn to be comfortable in **the life you create for yourself!**

Notes

4

| | 20 |
| | |

n	Mon	Tue	Wed	Thu	Fri	Sat
⌐	⌐	⌐	⌐	⌐	⌐	⌐
⌐	⌐	⌐	⌐	⌐	⌐	⌐
⌐	⌐	⌐	⌐	⌐	⌐	⌐
⌐	⌐	⌐	⌐	⌐	⌐	⌐
⌐	⌐	⌐	⌐	⌐	⌐	⌐
t a od eal	Tell someone something you've been holding on to this week	Sleep for 7 hours	Only speak in the positive and say positive things today	Drink your body weight in oz of H2O	Be vulnerable today	Safely indulge in one thing you want today

his month's mantra:

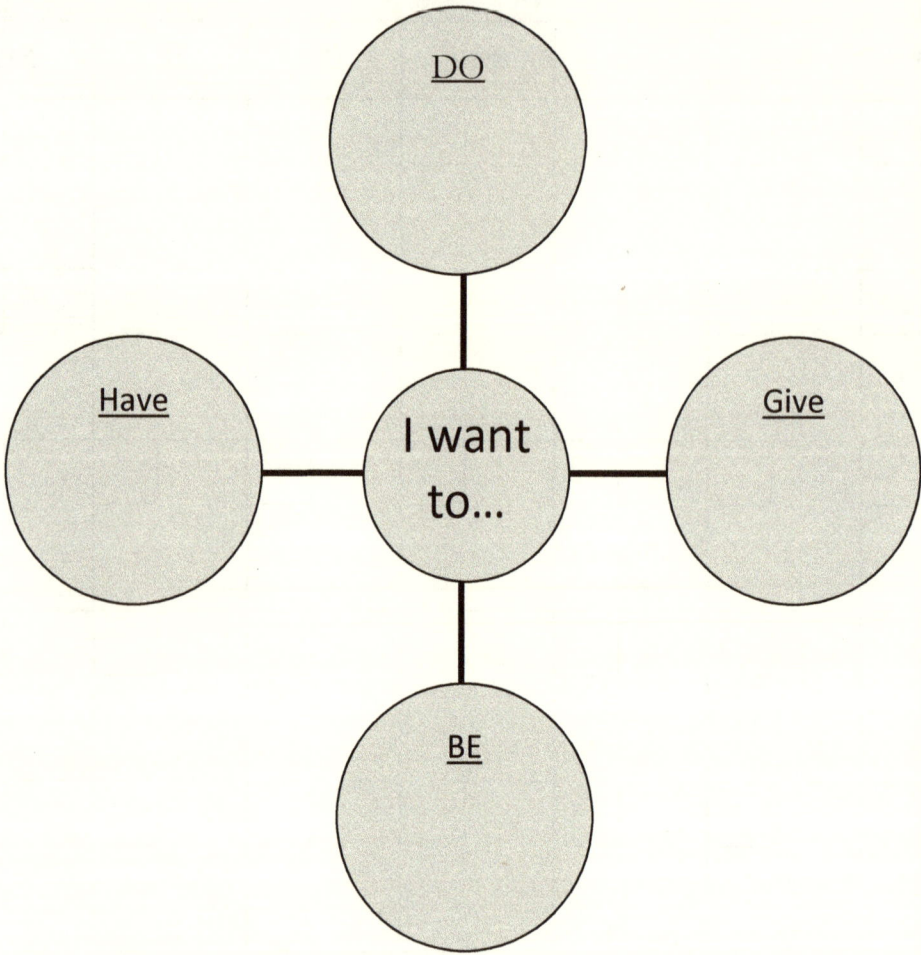

DO

Have

I want to...

Give

BE

This month's goals:

_____
_____
_____
_____
_____

1	_____
	_____
Day	_____
	_____
2	_____
	_____
Day	_____
	_____
3	_____
	_____
Day	_____
	_____
4	_____
	_____
Day	_____
	_____
5	_____
	_____
Day	_____
	_____
6	_____
	_____
Day	_____
	_____
7	_____
	_____
Day	_____

Daily Affirmations Complete? ☐

Jeremiah 17:7-8
New International Version (NIV)

"**7**But blessed is the one who trusts in the LORD, whose confidence is in him. **8** They will be like a tree planted by the water that sends out its roots by the stream. It does not fear when heat comes; its leaves are always green. It has no worries in a year of drought and never fails to bear fruit."

This week I'm going to/did _____ for my
Body:
Mind:
Peace:
Family:
Home:
World:

8	
Day	
9	
Day	
10	
Day	
11	
Day	
12	
Day	
13	
Day	
14	
Day	

Daily Affirmations Complete? ☐

This week I'm going to/did _____ for my
Body:
Mind:
Peace:
Family:
Home:
World:

ഔ൝

"Don't allow
your fear of
the worst to
keep you from
your best"

-Shannon C.

ഔ൝

15	
Day	
16	
Day	
17	
Day	
18	
Day	
19	
Day	
20	
Day	
21	
Day	

Daily Affirmations? ☐

Quality is not an act; it is a habit" -Aristotle

This week I'm going to/did _____ for my
Body:
Mind:
Peace:
Family:
Home:
World:

22	
DAY	
23	
DAY	
24	
DAY	
25	
DAY	
26	
DAY	
27	
DAY	
28	
DAY	

Daily Affirmations? ☐

This week I'm going to/did _____ for my		
Body:		
Mind:		
Peace:		
Family:		
Home:		
World:		

"Well done is better than well said"

-Benjamin Franklin

29	
Day	
30	
Day	
31	
Day	

Daily Affirmations? ☐

This Month's Take-Away:

Sun	Mon	Tue	Wed	Thu	Fri	Sa
⌐	⌐	⌐	⌐	⌐	⌐	
⌐	⌐	⌐	⌐	⌐	⌐	⌐
⌐	⌐	⌐	⌐	⌐	⌐	⌐
⌐	⌐	⌐	⌐	⌐	⌐	⌐
⌐	⌐	⌐	⌐	⌐	⌐	
Eat a good meal	Tell someone something you've been holding on to this week	Sleep for 7 hours	Only speak in the positive and say positive things today	Drink your body weight in oz of H2O	Be vulnerable today	Safe indulg one th you w toda

This month's mantra:

DO

Have

I want
to...

Give

BE

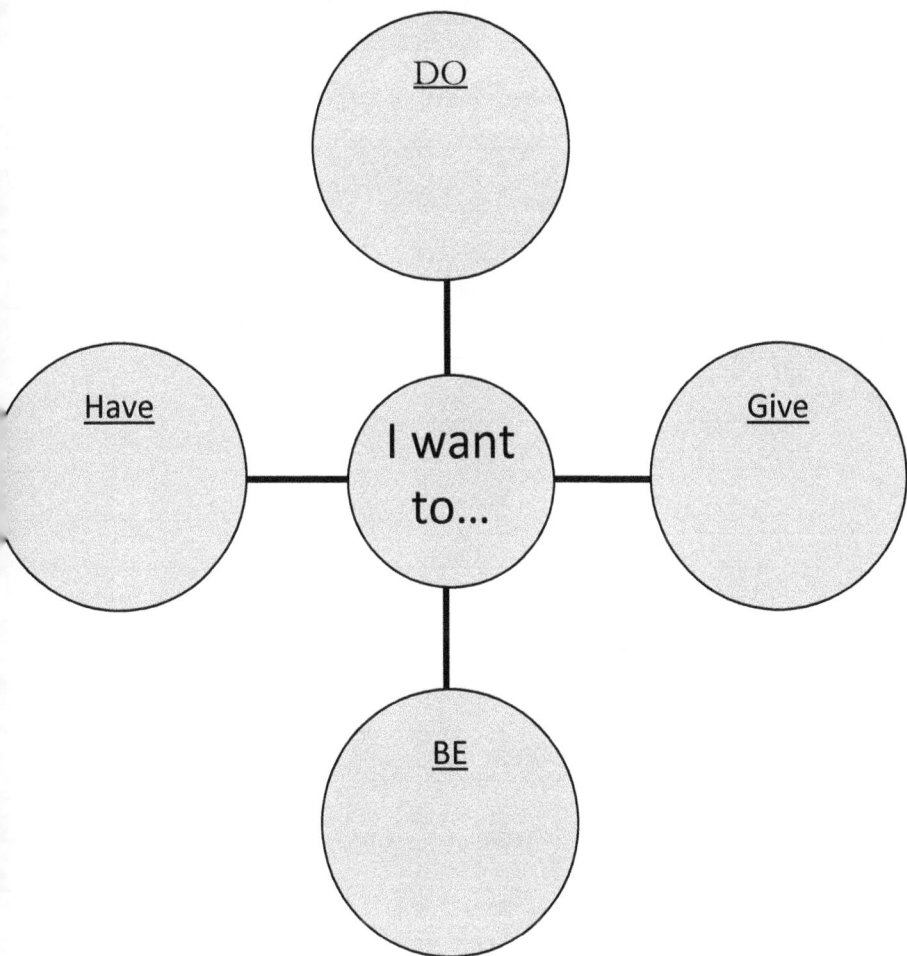

This month's goals

_____

_____

_____

_____

_____

1	
Day	
2	
Day	
3	
Day	
4	
Day	
5	
Day	
6	
Day	
7	
Day	

Daily Affirmations? ☐

Romans 12:9-11
King James Version (KJV)

"⁹ Let love be without dissimulation. Abhor that which is evil; cleave to that which is good.
¹⁰ Be kindly affectioned one to another with brotherly love; in honour preferring one another;
¹¹ Not slothful in business; fervent in spirit; serving the Lord..."

This week I'm going to/did _____ for my
Body:
Mind:
Peace:
Family:
Home:
World:

8	
Day	
9	
Day	
10	
Day	
11	
Day	
12	
Day	
13	
Day	
14	
Day	

Daily Affirmations? ☐

ജ രു

"The will to win, the desire to succeed, the urge to reach your full potential…

These are the keys that will unlock the door to personal excellence."

-Confucius

ജ രു

This week I'm going to/did _____ for my
Body:
Mind:
Peace:
Family:
Home:
World:

15	
DAY	
16	
DAY	
17	
DAY	
18	
DAY	
19	
DAY	
20	
DAY	
21	
DAY	

Daily Affirmations? ☐

" The secret of getting ahead is getting started." —Mark Twain

This week I'm going to/did _____ for my
Body:
Mind:
Peace:
Family:
Home:
World:

22	
Day	
23	
Day	
24	
Day	
25	
Day	
26	
Day	
27	
Day	
28	
Day	

Daily Affirmations?

This week I'm going to/did _____ for my
Body:
Mind:
Peace:
Family:
Home:
World:

"People often say that motivation doesn't last. Well, neither does bathing—that's why we recommend it daily."

-Zig Ziglar

29	
Day	
30	
Day	
31	
Day	

Daily Affirmations? ☐

This Month's Take-Away:

un	Mon	Tue	Wed	Thu	Fri	Sat
⌐	⌐	⌐	⌐	⌐	⌐	⌐
⌐	⌐	⌐	⌐	⌐	⌐	⌐
⌐	⌐	⌐	⌐	⌐	⌐	⌐
⌐	⌐	⌐	⌐	⌐	⌐	⌐
⌐	⌐	⌐	⌐	⌐	⌐	⌐
at a ood eal	Tell someone something you've been holding on to this week	Sleep for 7 hours	Only speak in the positive and say positive things today	Drink your body weight in oz of H20	Be vulnerable today	Safely indulge in one thing you want today

his month's mantra:

DO

Have

I want to...

Give

BE

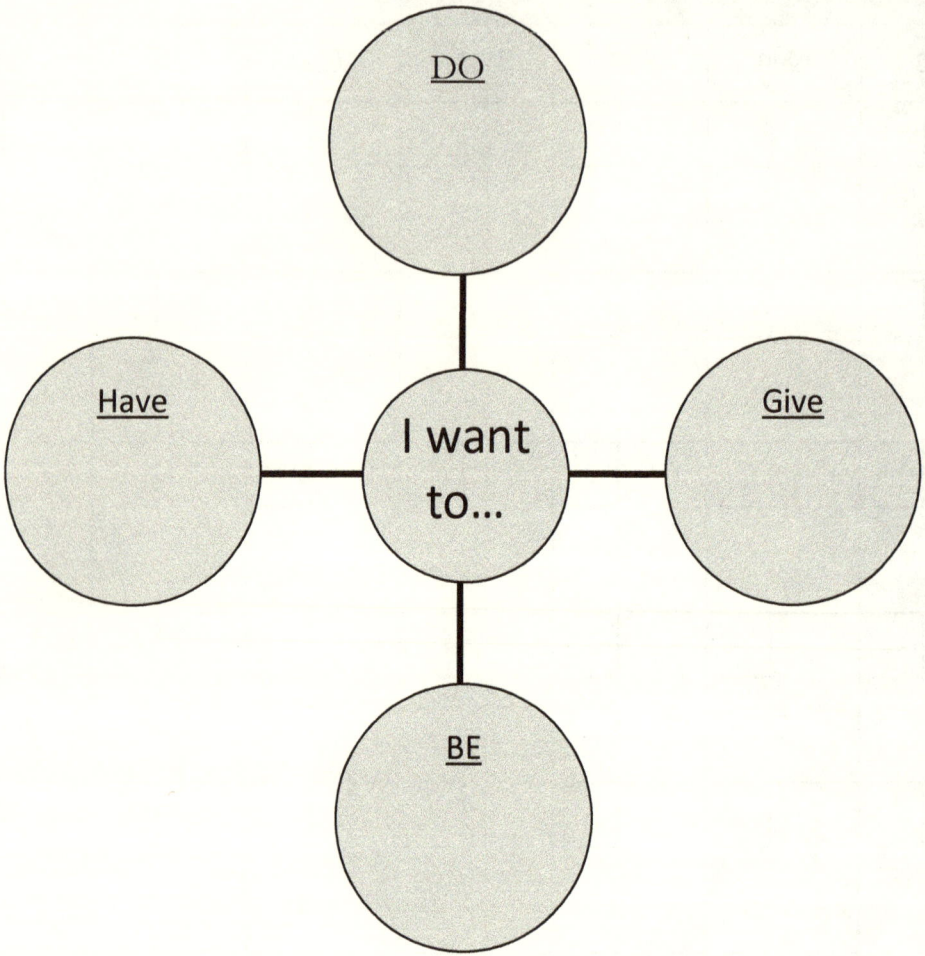

This month's goals

_____

_____

_____

_____

_____

1	
Day	
2	
Day	
3	
Day	
4	
Day	
5	
Day	
6	
Day	
7	
Day	

Daily Affirmations? □

Proverbs 31:25-7
King James Version (KJV)

[25] "Strength and honour are her clothing; and she shall rejoice in time to come. [26] She openeth her mouth with wisdom; and in her tongue is the law of kindness. [27] She looketh well to the ways of her household, and eateth not the bread of idleness."

This week I'm going to/did _____ for my	
Body:	
Mind:	
Peace:	
Family:	
Home:	
World:	

8	
Day	
9	
Day	
10	
Day	
11	
Day	
12	
Day	
13	
Day	
14	
Day	

Daily Affirmations? ☐

ജ୨ରଃ

"Accountability
breeds
response-
ability."

-Stephen Covey

ജ୨ରଃ

This week I'm going to/did _____ for my

Body:

Mind:

Peace:

Family:

Home:

World:

15	
Day	
16	
Day	
17	
Day	
18	
Day	
19	
Day	
20	
Day	
21	
Day	

Daily Affirmations? ☐

" Life is not easy for any of us. But what of that? We must have perseverance and above all confidence in ourselves. We must believe that we are gifted for something and that this thing must be attained. "

-Marie Curie

This week I'm going to/did _____ for my
Body:
Mind:
Peace:
Family:
Home:
World:

22	
Day	
23	
Day	
24	
Day	
25	
Day	
26	
Day	
27	
Day	
28	
Day	

Daily Affirmations? ☐

This week I'm going to/did _____ for my
Body:
Mind:
Peace:
Family:
Home:
World:

"Kindness in words creates confidence. Kindness in thinking creates profoundness. Kindness in giving creates love."

-Lao Tzu

29	
Day	
30	
Day	
31	
Day	

Daily Affirmations? ☐

This Month's Take-Away:

						20

Sun	Mon	Tue	Wed	Thu	Fri	Sa
Eat a good meal	Tell someone something you've been holding on to this week	Sleep for 7 hours	Only speak in the positive and say positive things today	Drink your body weight in oz of H2O	Be vulnerable today	Safe indul_ one th you w toda

This month's mantra:

38

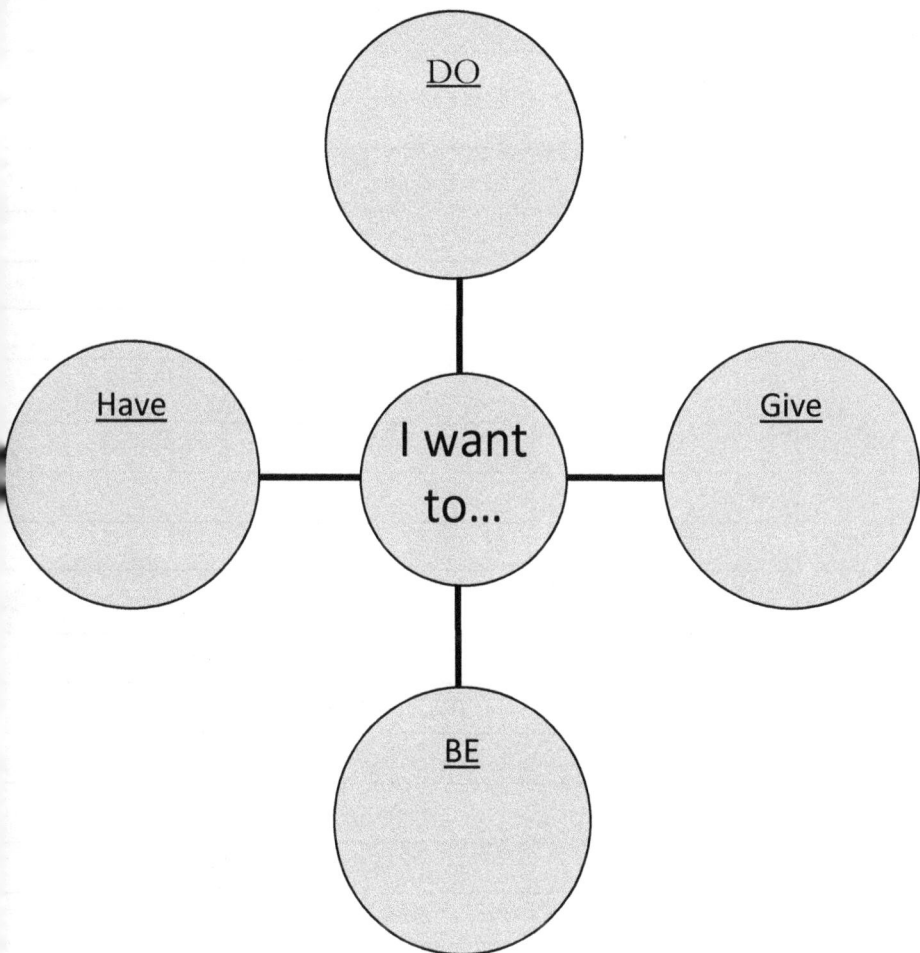

DO

Have

Give

I want to...

BE

This month's goals

_____

_____

_____

_____

_____

1	
Day	
2	
Day	
3	
Day	
4	
Day	
5	
Day	
6	
Day	
7	
Day	

Daily Affirmations? ☐

Isaiah 40:31
King James Version
(KJV)

"[31] But they that wait upon the LORD shall renew their strength; they shall mount up with wings as eagles; they shall run, and not be weary; and they shall walk, and not faint."

This week I'm going to/did _____ for my
Body:
Mind:
Peace:
Family:
Home:
World:

8	
DAY	
9	
DAY	
10	
DAY	
11	
DAY	
12	
DAY	
13	
DAY	
14	
DAY	

Daily Affirmations? ☐

42

ℰᖇ

"If I didn't define myself for myself, I would be crunched into other people's fantasies for me and eaten alive."

-Audre Lorde

ℰᖇ

This week I'm going to/did _____ for my
Body:
Mind:
Peace:
Family:
Home:
World:

15	
DAY	
16	
DAY	
17	
DAY	
18	
DAY	
19	
DAY	
20	
DAY	
21	
DAY	

Daily Affirmations? ☐

" I' m thankful to all those that said ' NO' because of them, I did it myself. "

—Albert Einstein

This week I'm going to/did _____ for my
Body:
Mind:
Peace:
Family:
Home:
World:

22	
Day	
23	
Day	
24	
Day	
25	
Day	
26	
Day	
27	
Day	
28	
Day	

Daily Affirmations? ☐

This week I'm going to/did _____ for my
Body:
Mind:
Peace:
Family:
Home:
World:

"My mother said to me, 'If you are a soldier, you will become a general. If you are a monk, you will become the Pope.' Instead I was a painter, and became Picasso."

-Pablo Picasso

29	
Day	
30	
Day	
31	
Day	

Daily Affirmations? ☐

This Month's Take-Away:

						20
un	**Mon**	**Tue**	**Wed**	**Thu**	**Fri**	**Sat**
at a ood eal	Tell someone something you've been holding on to this week	Sleep for 7 hours	Only speak in the positive and say positive things today	Drink your body weight in oz of H2O	Be vulnerable today	Safely indulge in one thing you want today

This month's mantra:

DO

Have

I want to...

Give

BE

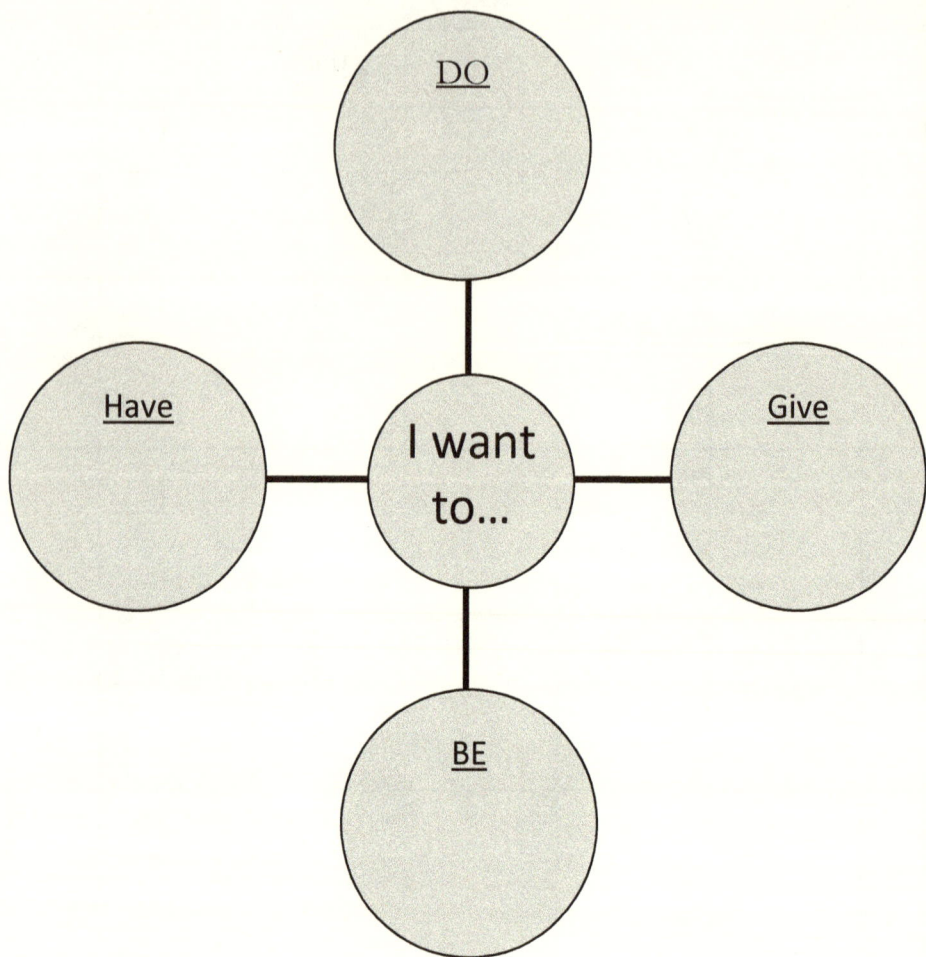

This month's goals

_____

_____

_____

_____

_____

1	
Day	
2	
Day	
3	
Day	
4	
Day	
5	
Day	
6	
Day	
7	
Day	

Daily Affirmations? ☐

Romans 12:2 King
James Version (KJV)

"2 And be not conformed to this world: but be ye transformed by the renewing of your mind, that ye may prove what is that good, and acceptable, and perfect, will of God."

This week I'm going to/did _____ for my
Body:
Mind:
Peace:
Family:
Home:
World:

8	
DAY	
9	
DAY	
10	
DAY	
11	
DAY	
12	
DAY	
13	
DAY	
14	
DAY	

Daily Affirmations? ☐

ഇ൰ൠ

" Don't worry about failures, worry about the chances you miss when you don't even try."

–Jack Canfield

ഇ൰ൠ

For My	
Body:	
Mind:	
Peace:	
Family:	
Home:	
World:	

15	
Day	
16	
Day	
17	
Day	
18	
Day	
19	
Day	
20	
Day	
21	
Day	

Daily Affirmations? ☐

" Sometimes the hardest part of the journey is believing you are worth the trip " —Glenn Beck

This week I'm going to/did _____ for my	
Body:	
Mind:	
Peace:	
Family:	
Home:	
World:	

22	
DAY	
23	
DAY	
24	
DAY	
25	
DAY	
26	
DAY	
27	
DAY	
28	
DAY	

Daily Affirmations? ☐

This week I'm going to/did _____ for my
Body:
Mind:
Peace:
Family:
Home:
World:

"Fill your brain with GIANT dreams so it has no room for petty pursuits."

-Robin Sharma

29	
Day	
30	
Day	
31	
Day	

Daily Affirmations? ☐

This Month's Take-Away:

Sun	Mon	Tue	Wed	Thu	Fri	S:
Eat a good meal	Tell someone something you've been holding on to this week	Sleep for 7 hours	Only speak in the positive and say positive things today	Drink your body weight in oz of H20	Be vulnerable today	Saf indul one t you tod

This month's mantra:

DO

Have

I want
to...

Give

BE

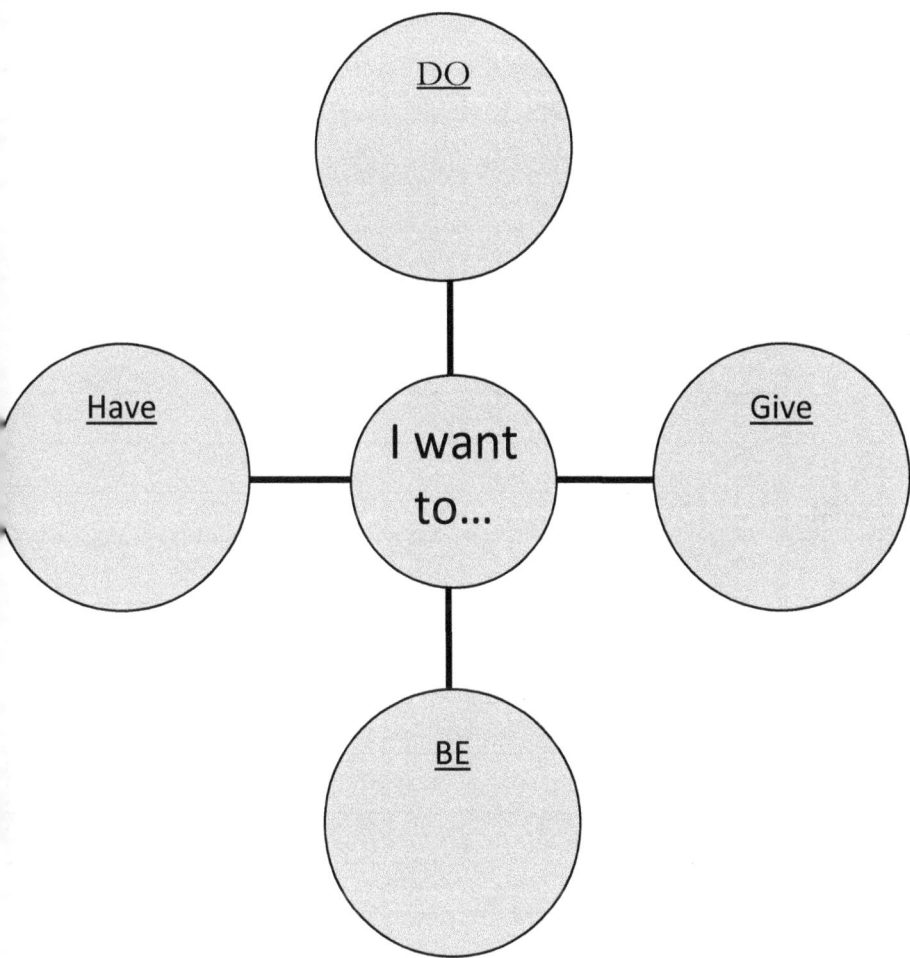

This month's goals

_____
_____
_____
_____
_____

1	
Day	
2	
Day	
3	
Day	
4	
Day	
5	
Day	
6	
Day	
7	
Day	

Daily Affirmations? ☐

Job 42:10
King James Version (KJV)

"**10** And the LORD turned the captivity of Job, when he prayed for his friends: also the LORD gave Job twice as much as he had before."

This week I'm going to/did _____ for my		
Body:		
Mind:		
Peace:		
Family:		
Home:		
World:		

8	
Day	
9	
Day	
10	
Day	
11	
Day	
12	
Day	
13	
Day	
14	
Day	

Daily Affirmations? ☐

This week I'm going to/did _____ for my

Body:

Mind:

Peace:

Family:

Home:

World:

ʂↄↄↄ

"Part of being successful is about asking questions and listening to the answers."

-Anne Burrell

ʂↄↄↄ

15	
Day	
16	
Day	
17	
Day	
18	
Day	
19	
Day	
20	
Day	
21	
Day	

Daily Affirmations?

" I have never developed indigestion from eating my words. "

—Winston Churchill

This week I'm going to/did _____ for my
Body:
Mind:
Peace:
Family:
Home:
World:

22	
Day	
23	
Day	
24	
Day	
25	
Day	
26	
Day	
27	
Day	
28	
Day	

Daily Affirmations? ☐

This week I'm going to/did _____ for my
Body:
Mind:
Peace:
Family:
Home:
World:

"Eating is so intimate. It's very sensual. When you invite someone to sit at your table and you want to cook for them, you're inviting a person into your life."

-Maya Angelou

29	
Day	
30	
Day	
31	
Day	

Daily Affirmations? ▢

This Month's Take-Away:

un	Mon	Tue	Wed	Thu	Fri	Sat
t a ꞏod eal	Tell someone something you've been holding on to this week	Sleep for 7 hours	Only speak in the positive and say positive things today	Drink your body weight in oz of H2O	Be vulnerable today	Safely indulge in one thing you want today

20

This month's mantra:

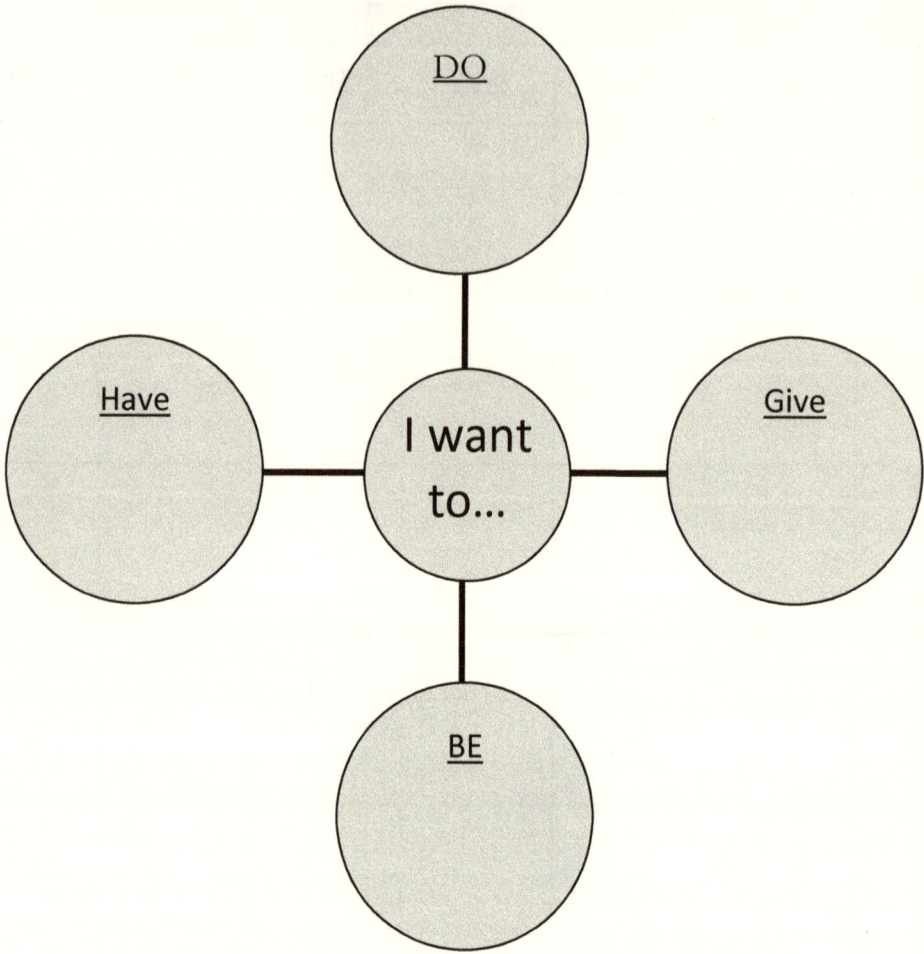

DO

Have

I want to...

Give

BE

This month's goals

_____

_____

_____

_____

_____

1	
Day	
2	
Day	
3	
Day	
4	
Day	
5	
Day	
6	
Day	
7	
Day	

Daily Affirmations? ☐

Exodus 4:10-12
King James Version (KJV)

"¹⁰ And Moses said unto the LORD, O my LORD, I am not eloquent, neither heretofore, nor since thou hast spoken unto thy servant: but I am slow of speech, and of a slow tongue.
¹¹ And the LORD said unto him, Who hath made man's mouth? or who maketh the dumb, or deaf, or the seeing, or the blind? have not I the LORD?
¹² Now therefore go, and I will be with thy mouth, and teach thee what thou shalt say."

This week I'm going to/did _____ for my
Body:
Mind:
Peace:
Family:
Home:
World:

8	
Day	
9	
Day	
10	
Day	
11	
Day	
12	
Day	
13	
Day	
14	
Day	

Daily Affirmations? ☐

ଶୀଓଓ

"The traveler sees what he sees, the tourist sees what he has come to see."

-Gilbert K. Chesterton

ଶୀଓଓ

This week I'm going to/did _____ for my
Body:
Mind:
Peace:
Family:
Home:
World:

15	
DAY	
16	
DAY	
17	
DAY	
18	
DAY	
19	
DAY	
20	
DAY	
21	
DAY	

Daily Affirmations? ☐

This week I'm going to/did _____ for my
Body:
Mind:
Peace:
Family:
Home:
World:

" I never travel without my diary. One should always have something sensational to read in the train. "

—Oscar Wilde

22	
DAY	
23	
DAY	
24	
DAY	
25	
DAY	
26	
DAY	
27	
DAY	
28	
DAY	

Daily Affirmations? ☐

This week I'm going to/did _____ for my
Body:
Mind:
Peace:
Family:
Home:
World:

"In order to heal others, we first need to heal ourselves. And to heal ourselves, we need to know how to deal with ourselves."

—Thich Nhat Hanh

29	
Day	
30	
Day	
31	
Day	

Daily Affirmations? ☐

This Month's Take-Away:

Sun	Mon	Tue	Wed	Thu	Fri	Sat
Eat a good meal	Tell someone something you've been holding on to this week	Sleep for 7 hours	Only speak in the positive and say positive things today	Drink your body weight in oz of H2O	Be vulnerable today	Safel indulg one thi you we toda

This month's mantra:

DO

Have

I want to...

Give

BE

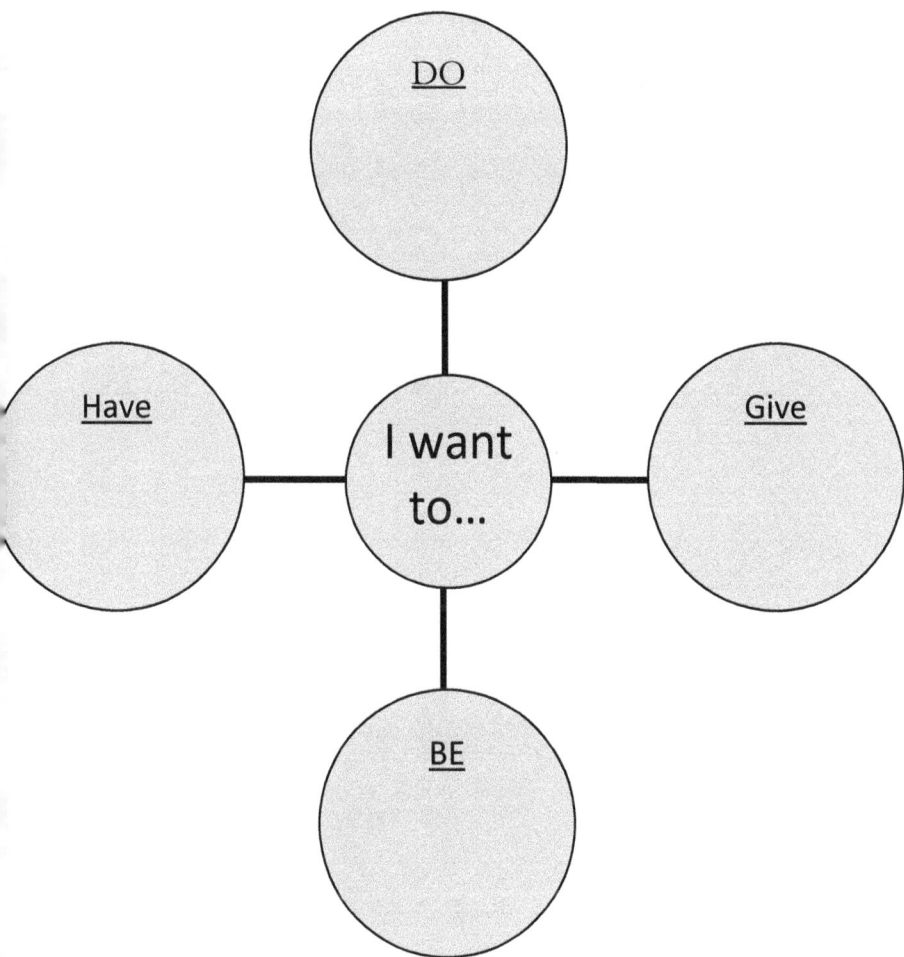

This month's goals

_____

_____

_____

_____

_____

1	
Day	
2	
Day	
3	
Day	
4	
Day	
5	
Day	
6	
Day	
7	
Day	

Daily Affirmations? ☐

Genesis 49:15
King James Version (KJV)

"15 And he saw that rest
was good, and the land
that it was pleasant; and
bowed his shoulder to
bear, and became a
servant unto tribute."

For My	
Body:	
Mind:	
Peace:	
Family:	
Home:	
World:	

8	
Day	
9	
Day	
10	
Day	
11	
Day	
12	
Day	
13	
Day	
14	
Day	

Daily Affirmations? ☐

ℰℭ

"Without continual growth and progress, such words as improvement, achievement, and success have no meaning.

-Benjamin Franklin

ℰℭ

This week I'm going to/did _____ for my
Body:
Mind:
Peace:
Family:
Home:
World:

15	
Day	
16	
Day	
17	
Day	
18	
Day	
19	
Day	
20	
Day	
21	
Day	

Daily Affirmations?

This week I'm going to/did _____ for my
Body:
Mind:
Peace:
Family:
Home:
World:

" Being good in business is the most fascinating kind of art. Making money is art and working is art and good business is the best art. "

– Andy Warhol

22	
Day	
23	
Day	
24	
Day	
25	
Day	
26	
Day	
27	
Day	
28	
Day	

Daily Affirmations?

This week I'm going to/did _____ for my
Body:
Mind:
Peace:
Family:
Home:
World:

"Disneyland is a work of love. We didn't go into Disneyland just with the idea of making money."
-Walt Disney

29	
Day	
30	
Day	
31	
Day	

Daily Affirmations? [ ]

This Month's Take-Away:

Sun	Mon	Tue	Wed	Thu	Fri	Sat
Eat a good meal	Tell someone something you've been holding on to this week	Sleep for 7 hours	Only speak in the positive and say positive things today	Drink your body weight in oz of H2O	Be vulnerable today	Safely indulge in one thing you want today

This month's mantra:

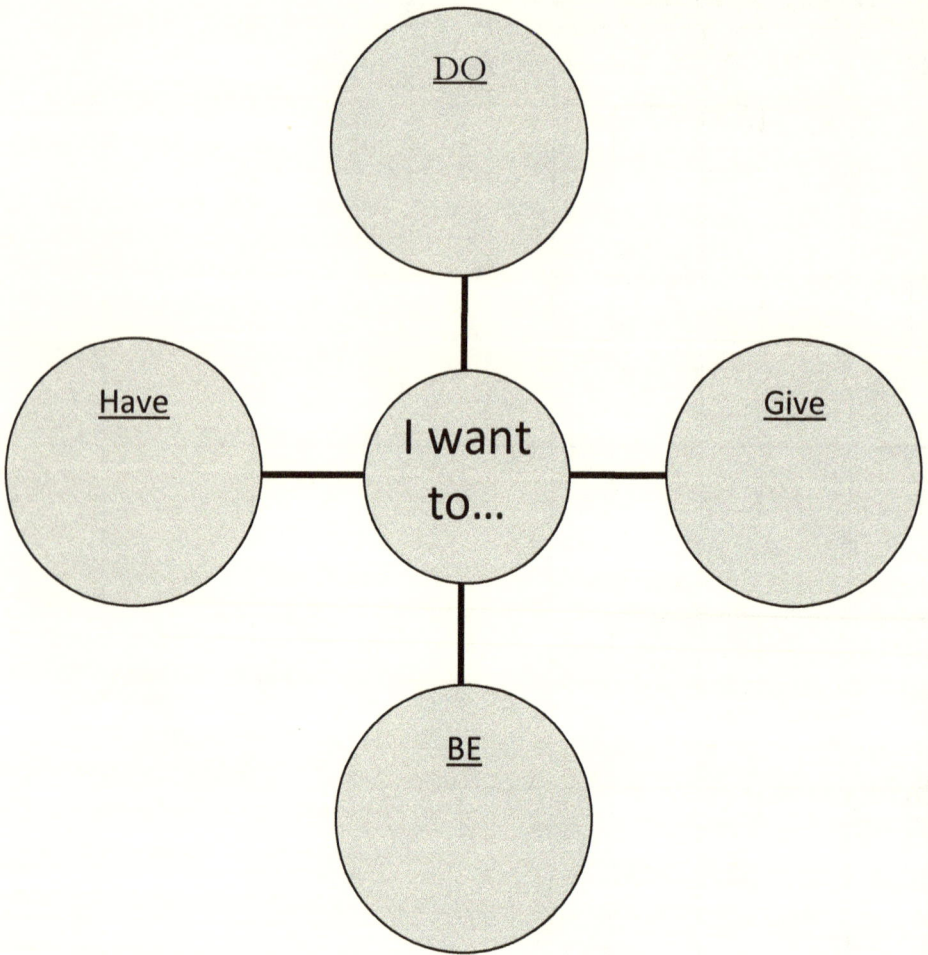

DO

Have

I want to...

Give

BE

This month's goals

_____

_____

_____

_____

_____

1	
Day	
2	
Day	
3	
Day	
4	
Day	
5	
Day	
6	
Day	
7	
Day	

Daily Affirmations? ☐

Psalm 59:9
King James Version (KJV)

"⁹ Because of his strength will I wait upon thee: for God is my defense."

This week I'm going to/did _____ for my
Body:
Mind:
Peace:
Family:
Home:
World:

8	
Day	
9	
Day	
10	
Day	
11	
Day	
12	
Day	
13	
Day	
14	
Day	

Daily Affirmations? ☐

ℰᑎᏏᎦ

"Don't be sorry, do better."

-Shannon Crutchfield

ℰᑎᏏᎦ

This week I'm going to/did _____ for my
Body:
Mind:
Peace:
Family:
Home:
World:

15	
DAY	
16	
DAY	
17	
DAY	
18	
DAY	
19	
DAY	
20	
DAY	
21	
DAY	

Daily Affirmations? ☐

" The real Antichrist is he who turns the wine of an original idea into the water of mediocrity. " - Eric Hoffer

This week I'm going to/did _____ for my

Body:

Mind:

Peace:

Family:

Home:

World:

22	
DAY	
23	
DAY	
24	
DAY	
25	
DAY	
26	
DAY	
27	
DAY	
28	
DAY	

Daily Affirmations? [ ]

This week I'm going to/did _____ for my
Body:
Mind:
Peace:
Family:
Home:
World:

"Don't respond to haters' taunts — even politely. Ignore them. If nobody takes their bait, most will grow bored and move on."

—Andrew Shaffer

29	
Day	
30	
Day	
31	
Day	

Daily Affirmations? ☐

This Month's Take-Away:

Sun	Mon	Tue	Wed	Thu	Fri	Sa
Eat a good meal	Tell someone something you've been holding on to this week	Sleep for 7 hours	Only speak in the positive and say positive things today	Drink your body weight in oz of H2O	Be vulnerable today	Saf indul one th you v tod

This month's mantra:

DO

Have

I want to...

Give

BE

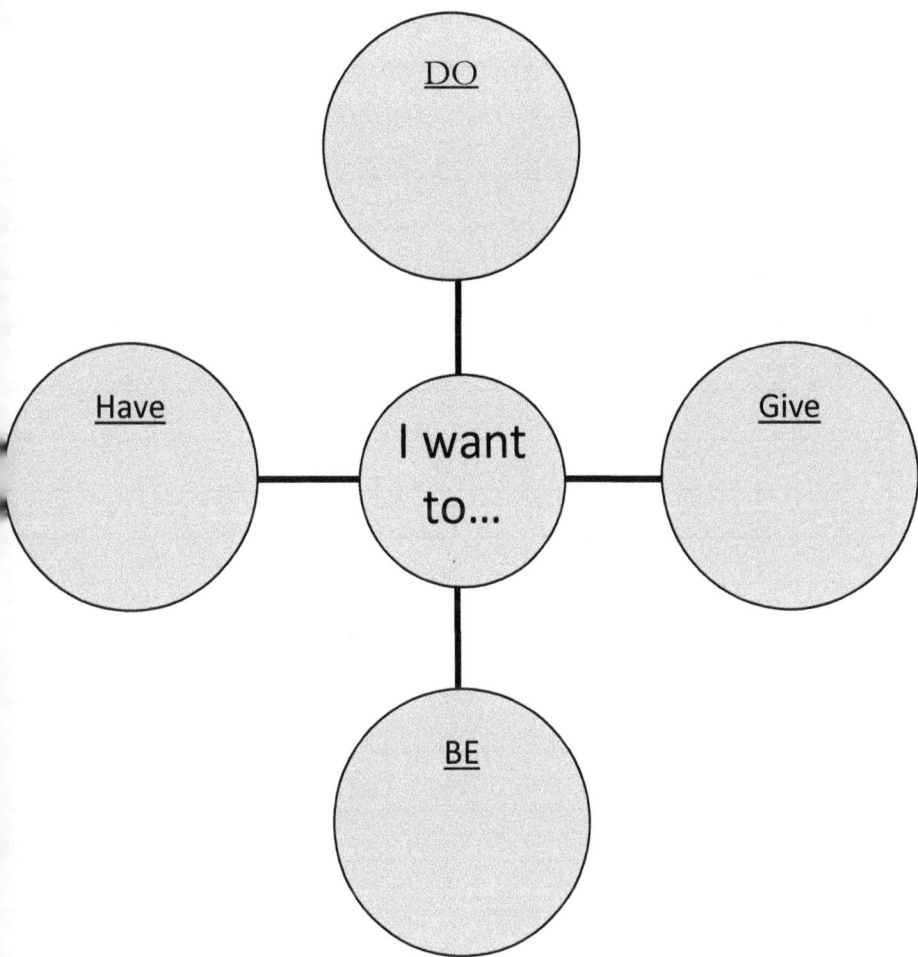

This month's goals

_____

_____

_____

_____

_____

1	
Day	
2	
Day	
3	
Day	
4	
Day	
5	
Day	
6	
Day	
7	
Day	

Daily Affirmations? ☐

1 Timothy 5:8
King James Version (KJV)

"8 But if any provide not for his own, and specially for those of his own house, he hath denied the faith, and is worse than an infidel."

This week I'm going to/did _____ for my
Body:
Mind:
Peace:
Family:
Home:
World:

8	
Day	
9	
Day	
10	
Day	
11	
Day	
12	
Day	
13	
Day	
14	
Day	

Daily Affirmations? ☐

ഇൗ

"I tend to gravitate to the darkest or most obscure part of any venue in an effort to have my own space to experience the music on my own, free from unwanted conversations and other distractions."

-Henry Rollins

ഇൗ

This week I'm going to/did _____ for my
Body:
Mind:
Peace:
Family:
Home:
World:

15	
Day	
16	
Day	
17	
Day	
18	
Day	
19	
Day	
20	
Day	
21	
Day	

Daily Affirmations? ☐

" Change will not come if we wait for some other person or some other time. We are the ones we've been waiting for. We are the change that we seek. " -Barack Obama

This week I'm going to/did _____ for my
Body:
Mind:
Peace:
Family:
Home:
World:

111

22	
Day	
23	
Day	
24	
Day	
25	
Day	
26	
Day	
27	
Day	
28	
Day	

Daily Affirmations? ☐

This week I'm going to/did _____ for my
Body:
Mind:
Peace:
Family:
Home:
World:

"The future rewards those who press on. I don't have time to feel sorry for myself. I don't have time to complain. I'm going to press on."

—Barak Obama

29	
Day	
30	
Day	
31	
Day	

Daily Affirmations? ☐

This Month's Take-Away:

...n	Mon	Tue	Wed	Thu	Fri	Sat
...t a ...od ...eal	Tell someone something you've been holding on to this week	Sleep for 7 hours	Only speak in the positive and say positive things today	Drink your body weight in oz of H2O	Be vulnerable today	Safely indulge in one thing you want today

This month's mantra:

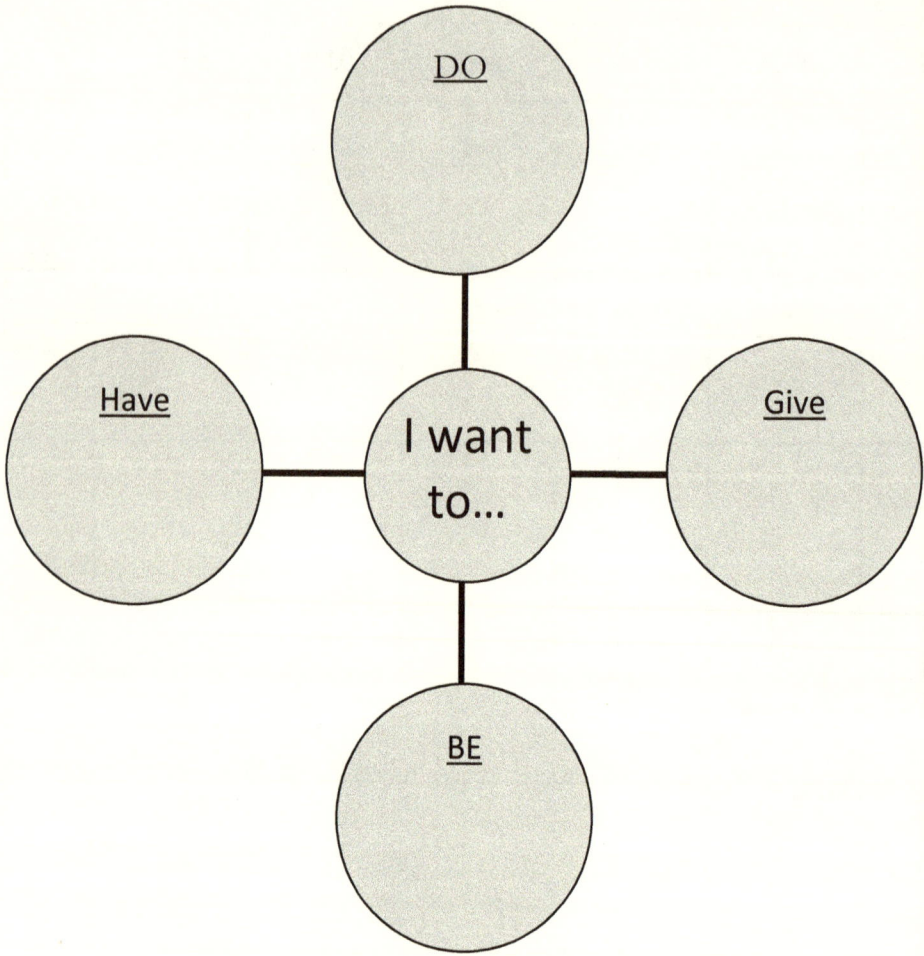

DO

Have

Give

I want to...

BE

This month's goals

_____

_____

_____

_____

_____

1	
Day	
2	
Day	
3	
Day	
4	
Day	
5	
Day	
6	
Day	
7	
Day	

Daily Affirmations? ☐

Deuteronomy 31:6
King James Version (KJV)

"⁶ Be strong and of a good courage, fear not, nor be afraid of them: for the LORD thy God, he it is that doth go with thee; he will not fail thee, nor forsake thee."

This week I'm going to/did _____ for my	
Body:	
Mind:	
Peace:	
Family:	
Home:	
World:	

8	
Day	
9	
Day	
10	
Day	
11	
Day	
12	
Day	
13	
Day	
14	
Day	

Daily Affirmations? ☐

This week I'm going to/did _____ for my

Body:

Mind:

Peace:

Family:

Home:

World:

ഓരു

"Daring to set boundaries is about having the courage to love ourselves, even when we risk disappointing others."

-Brene Brown

ഓരു

15	
Day	
16	
Day	
17	
Day	
18	
Day	
19	
Day	
20	
Day	
21	
Day	

Daily Affirmations? ☐

" One way to boost our will power and focus is to manage our distractions instead of letting them manage us. "
-Daniel Goleman

This week I'm going to/did _____ for my
Body:
Mind:
Peace:
Family:
Home:
World:

22	
Day	
23	
Day	
24	
Day	
25	
Day	
26	
Day	
27	
Day	
28	
Day	

Daily Affirmations?

This week I'm going to/did _____ for my
Body:
Mind:
Peace:
Family:
Home:
World:

"What you won't do is…Stop living because someone asked you to!!"

-Danielle Howard Ivory

29	
Day	
30	
Day	
31	
Day	

Daily Affirmations? ☐

This Month's Take-Away:

Sun	Mon	Tue	Wed	Thu	Fri	S
⌐	⌐	⌐	⌐	⌐	⌐	⌐
⌐	⌐	⌐	⌐	⌐	⌐	⌐
⌐	⌐	⌐	⌐	⌐	⌐	⌐
⌐	⌐	⌐	⌐	⌐	⌐	⌐
⌐	⌐	⌐	⌐	⌐	⌐	⌐
Eat a good meal	Tell someone something you've been holding on to this week	Sleep for 7 hours	Only speak in the positive and say positive things today	Drink your body weight in oz of H2O	Be vulnerable today	Say indul one t you too

20

This month's mantra:

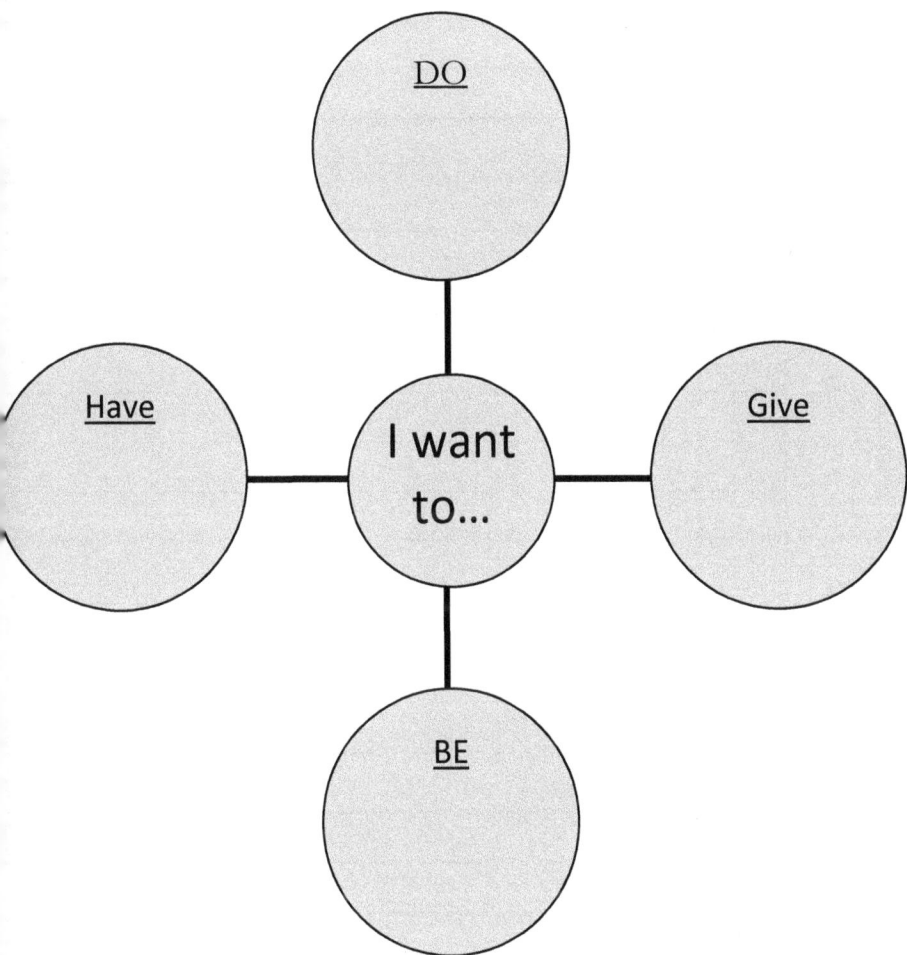

DO

Have

Give

I want to...

BE

This month's goals

_____
_____
_____
_____
_____

1	
Day	
2	
Day	
3	
Day	
4	
Day	
5	
Day	
6	
Day	
7	
Day	

Daily Affirmations? ☐

Jeremiah 17:14
King James Version (KJV)

"**14** Heal me, O LORD, and I shall be healed; save me, and I shall be saved: for thou art my praise."

This week I'm going to/did _____ for my
Body:
Mind:
Peace:
Family:
Home:
World:

8	
Day	
9	
Day	
10	
Day	
11	
Day	
12	
Day	
13	
Day	
14	
Day	

Daily Affirmations? □

 ℂℂ

"There never will
be complete
equality until
women
themselves help
to make laws
and elect
lawmakers."

-Susan B.
Anthony

 ℂℂ

This week I'm going to/did _____ for my

Body:

Mind:

Peace:

Family:

Home:

World:

15	
Day	
16	
Day	
17	
Day	
18	
Day	
19	
Day	
20	
Day	
21	
Day	

Daily Affirmations? ☐

This week I'm going to/did _____ for my
Body:
Mind:
Peace:
Family:
Home:
World:

22	
DAY	
23	
DAY	
24	
DAY	
25	
DAY	
26	
DAY	
27	
DAY	
28	
DAY	

Daily Affirmations? ☐

This week I'm going to/did _____ for my
Body:
Mind:
Peace:
Family:
Home:
World:

"You, yourself, as much as anybody in the entire universe, deserve your love and affection."
-Buddha

29	
Day	
30	
Day	
31	
Day	

Daily Affirmations? ☐

This Month's Take-Away:

n	Mon	Tue	Wed	Thu	Fri	Sat
⌐	⌐	⌐	⌐	⌐	⌐	⌐
⌐	⌐	⌐	⌐	⌐	⌐	⌐
⌐	⌐	⌐	⌐	⌐	⌐	⌐
⌐	⌐	⌐	⌐	⌐	⌐	⌐
⌐	⌐	⌐	⌐	⌐	⌐	⌐
: a ɔd al	Tell someone something you've been holding on to this week	Sleep for 7 hours	Only speak in the positive and say positive things today	Drink your body weight in oz of H2O	Be vulnerable today	Safely indulge in one thing you want today

"Let us always meet each other with smile, for the smile is the beginning of love."

-Mother Teresa

Hopefully you are smiling because you've ordered your journal for next year already.

Thank you for spending some time with so many others getting to not only know themselves but coming to love that person they discover even more! You can start these activities any day of the year at any time, but why not start right now, and be

"Day One Crazy"?!

www.ingramcontent.com/pod-product-compliance
Lightning Source LLC
Chambersburg PA
CBHW030510100426
42813CB00002B/413